SOCIAL
SECURITY

SOCIAL SECURITY

A Play in Two Acts
by

Andrew Bergman

NELSON DOUBLEDAY, INC.
Garden City, New York

For Jacob and Teddy

SOCIAL SECURITY by Andrew Bergman opened in New York City at The Ethel Barrymore Theatre on April 17, 1986, with the following cast:

DAVID KAHN	Ron Silver
BARBARA KAHN	Marlo Thomas
TRUDY HEYMAN	Joanna Gleason
MARTIN HEYMAN	Kenneth Welsh
SOPHIE GREENGRASS	Olympia Dukakis
MAURICE KOENIG	Stefan Schnabel

The production was directed by Mike Nichols. The setting was by Tony Walton, lighting was by Marilyn Rennagel, costumes were by Ann Roth, sound was by Otts Munderloh, and Peter Lawrence was the production stage manager.

SOCIAL
SECURITY

CHARACTERS

David Kahn
Barbara Kahn
Trudy Heyman
Martin Heyman
Sophie Greengrass
Maurice Koenig

ACT ONE

The Kahn Apartment on New York's East Side in the early evening. The present.

ACT TWO

SCENE ONE

The same room. Early evening, two weeks later.

SCENE TWO

The same room. Early Sunday afternoon, one week later.

ACT ONE

ACT I

SCENE ONE

The apartment of David and Barbara Kahn on the East Side of Manhattan, close to the park.

It is a third-floor apartment—a huge, high-ceilinged, grand New York home, remodeled to the point of unrecognizability. Curved rosewood and glass brick walls have replaced the thick plaster walls—in some cases cutting through the old ceiling moldings. Only the original doorman buzzer remains from the old apartment. Everything else has been transformed into a lush, modern showplace for the Kahns' art dealership. The design of the apartment is so strict that anything, anything out of place is a disaster.

The front door is downstage right and is flanked by a coat closet. Between the two doors is a large blue painting. Upstage right is a galley kitchen, with a service exit at its extreme end. Upstage center is a bookcase-lined hallway leading to David and Barbara's bedroom. Upstage left is David's marble desk, covered with art auction brochures. Above the desk is a large white painting. Stage left is an ornately carved bar, behind which is a rosewood column containing not only bar ware, but stereo equipment.

Downstage left is a huge window looking out onto gorgeous brownstone buildings across the street. In front of the window is a dining table and four chairs. Extreme downstage left is a door leading to a guest bedroom.

From any point in the apartment, one must take a large step down into the living room area.

3

It is early evening.

David Kahn is speaking on the telephone.

DAVID: *(Into the telephone)* Jack, forget it . . . *forget* it. Sure Enrico's gifted, that's not my point. My point is, are these paintings going to sell on Fifty-seventh Street, and my best judgment has to be, no. What does Barbara think? *(Calling off to the kitchen)* Honey, Jack wants to know what you think.

BARBARA: *(From the kitchen)* I think they're godawful, and you can quote me.

DAVID: "Godawful," and you can quote her.

(Barbara Kahn, fortyish, pearls and silk dress, enters from the kitchen carrying Brie and crackers on a tray)

DAVID: Sure, they're brilliant technically; nobody denies that Enrico's a great technician.

BARBARA: But the subject matter. *Please.*

DAVID: *(Covering phone, to Barbara)* Enrico had a rough summer. His wife left him . . . then came back.

BARBARA: But *still.* Canvas after canvas of dead chihuahuas. Lying on their little backs, their tongues black and protruding. I mean, what's the *point?*

DAVID: *(Into phone)* Jack, renaming the pictures isn't going to help. *Requiem for Chico One Through Twenty* is a perfectly legitimate title.

4

BARBARA: This is so ridiculous. *(Points to watch, indicating David should get off)*

DAVID: Jack, I'm going to have to run. You did your best, but no cigar. Right. . . . My best to Enrico.

BARBARA: And love from me. He shouldn't take it personally.

DAVID: And love from Barbara; you shouldn't take it personally. Right. *(Hangs up phone) God.*

BARBARA: He took it personally.

DAVID: Of course. He always does. *(Observes Barbara)* Can I ask why you're running around like a dervish?

BARBARA: You know exactly why. David, why do you think they're coming?

DAVID: I haven't the faintest idea. You spoke to Trudy. What did she say?

BARBARA: She said, "Martin and I would like to come over around seven and discuss something."

DAVID: So there we are. I'm sure it's nothing major. . . .

BARBARA: They're coming in from the Island. You know how much they hate coming in from the Island.

DAVID: Maybe they're going to the theater.

BARBARA: They never go to the theater. Not unless *Fiddler* is playing somewhere. Think for a second, what could they want to discuss with us?

DAVID: Is the gorgeous Sarah giving them trouble?

BARBARA: Not that I know of. She's apparently quite happy in Buffalo.

DAVID: She's in Buffalo already?

BARBARA: It's November. She's been there two months.

DAVID: Amazing. That kid in college. I remember holding her in my lap.

BARBARA: Me, too. At Mother's party last April.

DAVID: I couldn't resist. Martin was ready to kill me.

BARBARA: God, what do they want? This is so unlike them.

DAVID: My guess is, they just decided to spend an evening out and wanted to drop by.

BARBARA: "Discuss something," is what she said.

DAVID: Maybe they want us to kick in a little more for your mother.

BARBARA: Trudy would have said so over the phone. She's never been shy about money.

6

DAVID: *(Crossing to the bar)* Do you want a drink?

BARBARA: No, thank you.

DAVID: Me either. We don't really deserve this bar. Look at this—Evian water, Pellegrino water. . . . William Powell must be turning in his grave.

BARBARA: I don't believe William Powell ever owned this bar.

DAVID: The architect swore.

BARBARA: He swore a lot of things. We should have framed that estimate. We could have sold it as an abstract expressionist.

DAVID: *(After a beat)* You hear from him?

BARBARA: Do I hear from whom?

DAVID: From whom? You know who. That draftsman he had up here.

BARBARA: Richard.

DAVID: Richard.

BARBARA: No. Why should I hear from him? *(David shrugs)* Oh, please.

DAVID: Hey, I didn't say . . .

BARBARA: You want to believe something happened, go ahead. This is like a club you take out every six months to whack me over the head with. We had lunch. He was adorable. And that was that. *(Emphatic)* Nothing . . . happened. You should talk.

DAVID: I should talk? Are we going to have a whole thing now?

BARBARA: That Italian sculptress came in yesterday, Miss Bazooms. It was a joke.

DAVID: I have to flirt. They expect it.

BARBARA: *Please.* It was like a B movie. And I'm standing right there.

DAVID: It's called professional charm.

BARBARA: You call it professional charm.

DAVID: I'm sorry. Really. I had no idea what she was going to look like. Then she came in, with that blouse . . .

BARBARA: Was that actually a blouse? It was hard to tell.

DAVID: Sorry. Really.

BARBARA: Yeah . . .

DAVID: I'm starving. Where are we going to eat?

BARBARA: I thought La Goulue.

DAVID: Great. Who are we eating with?

Act One

BARBARA: Trudy and Martin.

DAVID: God. Do we have to *eat* with them?

BARBARA: Yes. If they want to discuss something, it's always easier over a good meal.

DAVID: You don't even know what they want to discuss.

BARBARA: I'm sure it's serious. Trudy sounded so . . .

DAVID: Unhappy?

BARBARA: No, not unhappy.

DAVID: Upset?

BARBARA: Not really.

DAVID: Euphoric? Giddy?

BARBARA: Strict.

DAVID: Strict?

BARBARA: Stern. Sober. She sounded like a prisoner of war reading from a prepared statement.

DAVID: What did she actually say?

BARBARA: Her exact words?

DAVID: Doesn't have to be verbatim.

9

BARBARA: It opened, "Hello, Barbara? Trudy." Then the usual, "How's David? How's Martin?" And so on.

DAVID: Then?

BARBARA: Then she said, quite out of the blue, "Are you and David planning on being home tonight?" I said, "Sure, it's just a regular old Tuesday night." Then she said, "You don't have one of your *openings* to attend tonight?" *"Openings,"* that's just how she said it, like it was something dirty.

DAVID: Putting you on the defensive.

BARBARA: Then she says, with this *voice*, "You sure you're not having some trendy little East Side dinner?"

DAVID: This is nothing new.

BARBARA: She has this view of us; it's so *depressing* to me. Then she completes it all by saying, "Because Martin and I have something we'd like to discuss with you and David. Alone." *Alone.* Think about it, David, I'm not seeing this clearly, I know."

DAVID: Sarah's knocked up. They want a trendy little East Side abortionist.

BARBARA: I keep thinking maybe Mother isn't well.

DAVID: If anything was wrong, Trudy would have told you over the phone.

10

BARBARA: *(Freezes, puts her hand over her heart)* Of course. Mother died. Oh my God, she died.

DAVID: Barbara, for crissakes, you don't come to someone's house to *discuss* the fact that your mother died. "We've got something we'd like to talk over with you, Barbara—and David, we'd like your opinion, too— Mother is dead."

BARBARA: I have a bad feeling.

DAVID: Your mother's barely eighty. She's got at least thirty years left.

BARBARA: Come on, David; she did break her hip.

DAVID: At a Macy's white sale.

BARBARA: So what? It's a sign.

DAVID: It's a sign she's not feeble. I mean, it's one thing to break your hip just rolling off the john. She was apparently *running* down the aisle toward some bath towels.

BARBARA: David, she's definitely deteriorating. Her hearing . . .

DAVID: She never listened anyhow. I'm telling you, they have some crisis with Sarah—a sex and/or drug scandal.

BARBARA: You know, I think you're rooting for that.

DAVID: Certainly not, but it is a possibility. Sarah's a spectacular, miraculous girl, raised by a pair of yaks. Now that she's left the nest, she wants to make herself over, create herself, screw lots and lots of people.

BARBARA: God, I hope not. They'd go crazy. *(She sighs, dramatically)*

DAVID: Why are you sighing? You're worrying yourself into this state.

BARBARA: You know, I haven't spoken to her in a week.

DAVID: Who?

BARBARA: Mother.

DAVID: It's no sin. We've been so busy.

BARBARA: We're always so busy.

DAVID: You do as well with your mother as can possibly be expected.

BARBARA: It's not enough.

DAVID: It's never enough.

(The intercom buzzer sounds, deafeningly. Barbara recoils)

BARBARA: God!

DAVID: *(Checks his watch)* On the button.

(The buzzer sounds again. Barbara rushes toward the intercom)

DAVID: When are they going to fix that thing?

BARBARA: *(Into intercom)* Yes?

DAVID: Like a goddamn air raid warning.

BARBARA: *(Into intercom)* What? Okay. Thank you.

DAVID: Them?

BARBARA: Them. *(Barbara opens the door, looks down the hall, closes the door)* I hate this. That interval after the buzzer sounds.

DAVID: It's in Dante. The ninth circle of hell. You spend eternity waiting by the door for someone to get off the elevator.

BARBARA: My palms always start to sweat. God, I hope it's nothing serious.

DAVID: Your palms? I'm sure they'll dry right up again.

BARBARA: David, I am not enjoying your humor this evening. Really. *(She opens the door and peers down the hall)* Hi! *(She closes the door again)* They're here.

DAVID: You going to make them ring the bell?

BARBARA: *(Opens the front door)* Hi! Welcome! Welcome!

TRUDY: Hello.

13

(Martin nods. Martin and Trudy Heyman enter. Trudy has a sensible, semistylish hairdo à la Geraldine Ferraro. Her clothes are similarly sensible and dull. Martin, bespectacled, trails behind his wife, looking very uncomfortable)

BARBARA: David . . . look who's here.

DAVID: *(Crossing to greet his in-laws)* Right on time, too. Martin and Trudy are the perfect guests. Hello, dear. *(David goes to kiss Trudy. She turns her head to avoid getting kisses on the mouth)* How are you. You look marvelous.

TRUDY: Thank you. I'm all right.

DAVID: Martin.

MARTIN: David. *(A manly handshake)*

DAVID: This a new suit I see?

MARTIN: This? No, I've had this suit, what, three years, Trudy?

TRUDY: Four years at least.

MARTIN: I think you're wrong. I think it's three.

TRUDY: *(Definitive)* Four. We were still driving the Valiant.

BARBARA: Well, three or four, it's a very nice suit. Glen plaid becomes you, Martin.

14

TRUDY: Your suit is something, David.

DAVID: Thank you. It's not new either, actually. . . .

(An awkward silence)

BARBARA: Well, let's not all stand around like it's some *cocktail* party. Sit, sit.

DAVID: Anybody care for a drink?

TRUDY: If you have ginger ale.

DAVID: One ginger ale. Martin, you're a Seven and Seven man, aren't you.

MARTIN: I never drink before eight.

BARBARA: Well, you can pretend.

MARTIN: I never pretend. Ginger ale is fine.

BARBARA: Two ginger ales. Fine. Please, everybody sit.

(Barbara and David both flee for the safety of the kitchen, but Barbara gets there first. David is left with his in-laws. Martin inspects the two canvases.

MARTIN: You haven't sold these yet, huh?

DAVID: No, I have a real soft spot for those, Martin.

15

MARTIN: I always forget those crazy names. What's this one called, the blue one?

DAVID: The Waldman? *Chesapeake Bay Variations.*

MARTIN: Uh, huh. And the other one is Long Island Sound, right? *(Martin laughs. Some laugh)*

DAVID: Good old Martin. No, the Ferragini is called *When Lilacs Bloomed.*

MARTIN: And you paid a thousand each for them?

DAVID: Correct.

MARTIN: And what are they worth today?

DAVID: Martin, every time you come here, you want to know what they're worth. It doesn't change that drastically from year to year. Over a span of years . . .

MARTIN: But it does change. I'm just curious, as an accountant, as someone interested in value, in appreciation and depreciation.

DAVID: Well, I'd say the Waldman is worth about eighteen thousand. Ferragini is a little out of vogue, I'm afraid, so I would guess *When Lilacs Bloomed* would go for around seven, eight thousand.

TRUDY: How can one be in vogue and the other one not? They're both blank.

DAVID: Well, they're not blank. There's paint on them. They're paintings.

MARTIN: But there's no picture.

TRUDY: I guess we don't understand art, Martin. David is an expert. He knows.

MARTIN: They're blank.

DAVID: Martin, I don't insist that you like these two paintings. Taste is, of course, a subjective matter. But please recognize that the paintings are not blank. One has modalities of blue; the other, white. The paint is thicker in some places, thinner in others. Both paintings have texture. They do not depict bowls of fruit, little blue boys, or lonesome choo–choos in the night. But they are paintings.

MARTIN: They're blank.

(Barbara enters from the kitchen with two glasses of ginger ale and coasters)

BARBARA: You aren't arguing about those paintings again?

DAVID: Martin continues to withhold his approval.

MARTIN: No, I approve that you paid two grand and now they're worth twenty-five. I think that's good business. I think as art they stink, and I'm not afraid to say it.

DAVID: You've never been afraid to say it.

BARBARA: Martin, sit. Here. *(She gestures to Martin to sit beside Trudy on the sofa. Then, to Trudy)* If the ginger ale isn't cold enough, I can get more ice.

TRUDY: Hot and cold are all the same to me.

MARTIN: Cheese and crackers.

DAVID: Do you eat cheese before eight?

BARBARA: David, don't be a tease.

TRUDY: Looks very nice.

MARTIN: What is this white cheese called?

BARBARA: Brie.

TRUDY: We've had that, Martin, at the Baumans'. It's unbelievably expensive.

BARBARA: Not really.

MARTIN: Have you ever seen two sisters so different? One says expensive; the other says cheap.

DAVID: They're like those paintings. I mean, they're similar in origin, but how come one goes up in value, while the other levels off? *(An awkward silence; Trudy munches some cheese)* That didn't come out right.

MARTIN: You think Trudy's leveled off?

18

BARBARA: Not at all. You look great, Trudy, and I'm not just saying that. Your hair, your skin . . .

DAVID: Absolutely. It was just a figure of speech—a metaphor, a simile. Whatever.

MARTIN: Excellent cheese. We should get this, Trudy.

TRUDY: It costs a fortune.

BARBARA: Trudy, I don't know where you get that idea.

TRUDY: All French cheese . . .

DAVID: We buy it on time, actually. Just a small down payment, then pennies a month. By the end of the year, the cheese is ours.

TRUDY: You can't keep it a year.

BARBARA: *(After a beat)* Martin, how's business with you?

TRUDY: He's so busy. He can hardly talk when I call.

DAVID: Is November busy for accountants? I think it'd be a slow period, before the tax season. . . .

MARTIN: I'm doing a lot of tax *planning* for clients these days. Retirement plans, IRAs . . .

TRUDY: He works like a dog.

MARTIN: . . . deferred annuities, pensions . . .

TRUDY: A dog. While I'm home with Mom.

BARBARA: Oh, Trudy, you know I meant to call Mom on Wednesday, but we had such a week at the gallery.

TRUDY: What else is new?

MARTIN: How's business with you, David?

DAVID: Quite good, actually, considering the weather's been so lousy.

MARTIN: That makes a difference?

DAVID: Not to some galleries, but we've always had a lot of street trade. Tourists, people just out for a stroll. You'd be surprised how many people just wander in and whip out a checkbook when they see something they like.

TRUDY: Can you imagine? People are such idiots.

DAVID: Art's a superb investment, Trudy, if you know what you're doing. Right now, for instance, we have a first show by a young Brazilian, Oliveros. . . .

BARBARA: He's wonderful. Even you two . . .

DAVID: Kind of Rousseauesque. Enormous moons, looming breasts. Everything larger than life. Fantastic color.

MARTIN: Expensive?

BARBARA: Not really.

20

TRUDY: To Barbara nothing is expensive.

BARBARA: Trudy, that's not fair. How can you say that?

TRUDY: How can I say that? In school who had to get a new loose-leaf binder every term? Me? No. I had the same one for four years. You, a new one every term.

BARBARA: That's because I wrote my boyfriend's name all over it, and I was changing boyfriends every term.

TRUDY: And I didn't have boyfriends?

BARBARA: I didn't say you didn't have boyfriends.

TRUDY: Jerry Lazar?

BARBARA: Of course, I remember Jerry Lazar.

MARTIN: Who is Jerry Lazar?

TRUDY: I told you about Jerry Lazar.

MARTIN: No, you didn't.

TRUDY: Of course I did.

DAVID: *(Rises)* I'll be at the table if anyone needs me.

(David sits at the dining table, out of the fray. Barbara leaps in)

BARBARA: Trudy, how's the volunteer work going?

21

DAVID: I didn't know Trudy does volunteer work.

BARBARA: Sure she does.

MARTIN: For years now. With the Brownies.

DAVID: Isn't that marvelous.

BARBARA: Still Mondays and Thursdays, Trude? I remember those pictures you showed me once. *(To David)* She had the most adorable group of little girls.

TRUDY: I quit.

BARBARA: You quit?

DAVID: Oh, no. That's a shocker.

TRUDY: I had no choice.

DAVID: The Brownies forced you out?

TRUDY: It was Mom.

BARBARA: Mom?

DAVID: How is your mother? I haven't spoken to her.

MARTIN: She's impossible.

TRUDY: She forced me out of the Brownies.

DAVID: That's unconscionable.

22

BARBARA: Trudy . . .

TRUDY: She didn't want me out of the house on Mondays and Thursdays.

BARBARA: You're home every other day.

TRUDY: Every goddamn day.

MARTIN: It's gotten very bad. We have a situation.

DAVID: I see.

TRUDY: She won't be left alone anymore. She refuses. I have to be there around the clock.

BARBARA: Get some help. We'll gladly pay for half, or three quarters.

DAVID: Whatever. Absolutely.

BARBARA: Trudy, is this what you wanted to discuss? Is it Mom? Because if it is, I've told you a hundred times, anything you want to do, just give me a call, I'll sit down and write you a check.

DAVID: Sky's the limit in that department.

(Trudy folds her hands; Barbara presses on)

BARBARA: I mean, is it this thing with the Brownies, Trudy, that you want to discuss? Because my opinion, for what it's worth—and you've got Mom, so I defer to you, because you're an absolute saint with her and she's

23

been so happy with you in Mineola—my opinion is, you get a girl to be with Mom twice a week, three times, whatever you want, and you go back to those Brownies, because I know how much that means to you.

DAVID: I could not agree more.

MARTIN: It's not that simple. This is a complicated issue. It affects Mom, it affects us . . . *(A significant beat)* . . . it affects you.

DAVID: Maybe the smallest drink wouldn't hurt. *(He sprints toward the bar)* Anyone else?

BARBARA: I'll take a straight scotch, dear.

TRUDY: Mom won't take any help. She has to be with her children.

BARBARA: But, Trudy, that's totally unreasonable. I mean, Christ . . .

MARTIN: You can't argue with her. She plays deaf.

DAVID: Write her notes.

BARBARA: David . . .

MARTIN: She won't read them. Trudy leaves her notes. She spits out those half-eaten sour balls in them. I've never known a person incapable of finishing a sour ball.

TRUDY: She goes through a can of them a day now. A can of half-eaten sour balls. And then she methodically leaves them all over the house. Planting them . . .

MARTIN: I found a green one in my wallet this morning.

TRUDY: I find them in the carpeting, on the stairs, in the toaster—burning, smoldering . . . it's a nightmare.

BARBARA: I would just insist—*insist*—on getting help.

TRUDY: You would "just insist"? Barbara, you have no idea what's going on with her.

DAVID: *(Returning from the bar with drinks for himself and Barbara)* Martin, Trudy, you sure . . . ?

TRUDY: We're fine. *(To Barbara)* Did I tell you about her long-distance calls?

BARBARA: No. Who does she know out of town?

TRUDY: Nobody. She makes mistakes. When she calls her friends in Manhattan, Mrs. Hirsch and Mrs. Lander, she dials 213 instead of 212.

DAVID: 213 is Los Angeles.

MARTIN: Our phone bill last month was over five hundred dollars.

BARBARA: Oh my God.

TRUDY: When they pick up, she starts talking. Sometimes we're lucky and they hang up. Other times, they put her on hold.

MARTIN: For a half hour, at day rates, she's conversing with some static in Beverly Hills.

BARBARA: Trudy, I feel so badly for you.

TRUDY: It's a complete disaster.

DAVID: Maybe if you knew where the calls were going to . . .

MARTIN: Of course. We got the phone statement; first thing, we tracked down the number.

BARBARA: Who's she been calling?

TRUDY: Twentieth Century-Fox.

DAVID: That's absurd. She should have her agent do that.

BARBARA: Why don't you dial for her, Trudy?

TRUDY: Why don't I dial for her? Because she doesn't want me dialing for her! She wants me chained to the kitchen, boiling her tea, making her those little whole wheat sandwiches.

BARBARA: Well, just put your foot down!

TRUDY: *(Getting up)* I've had it, Barb. I've absolutely had it! And the *last* thing I need is your advice!

BARBARA: Trudy!

MARTIN: *(To David)* It's been building up, the pressure. I mean, our married life . . .

DAVID: I understand.

MARTIN: Three years of it. And her mother's getting more difficult. There's a mean streak now. . . .

TRUDY: Our life is over!

BARBARA: Trudy.

TRUDY: We have nothing! Absolutely nothing! She's up at all hours, walking the halls, coughing.

DAVID: Well, you still have Sarah. I'm sure that's a great comfort.

BARBARA: Of course, you have Sarah.

TRUDY: We don't have Sarah anymore.

BARBARA: She went away to school. You might not have her in the physical, everyday sense. . . .

TRUDY: We lost her.

BARBARA: Trudy, if I do say so, you're being ridiculous. She's still your daughter. She'll be home on vacations.

MARTIN: She's gone. She's vanished.

27

DAVID: You mean she's literally a missing person?

MARTIN: In a sense.

DAVID: Martin, she's either missing or she's not missing. We're not having a metaphysical dialogue.

TRUDY: We have a problem with her. That's really why we came tonight, Barbara and David. That's really what we have to discuss.

DAVID: Don't hide anything from us. You know how we feel about Sarah.

MARTIN: *(Slowly; reluctantly)* We have a problem with her.

BARBARA: Academic problems?

(Trudy shakes her head)

DAVID: Something with drugs . . . or sex?

TRUDY: If we hadn't been stuck with Mom, we could have seen it coming, we could have done something.

MARTIN: I don't think so.

TRUDY: Of course we could have. Absolutely.

BARBARA: Trudy, what exactly . . .

TRUDY: Martin, tell them . . . tell my sophisticated sister and brother-in-law.

28

BARBARA: Trudy . . .

MARTIN: She's been upset. It's been a difficult week, since we found out.

DAVID: Martin, what precisely is the matter?

MARTIN: *(Exhales deeply)* Okay. The last couple of weeks, whenever we call Sarah at the dormitory . . .

BARBARA: Which is about how often?

TRUDY: Twice a day.

DAVID: Jesus H. Christ.

BARBARA: Twice a *day?*

TRUDY: *(To Martin)* I told you.

BARBARA: No, but really . . .

DAVID: Folks, you've got to give that kid some air.

TRUDY: She's our only child.

DAVID: That's not the point.

MARTIN: Forgive me, David, but you can't understand the strain, the worry. . . .

DAVID: Well, I can already imagine the payoff to this.

TRUDY: No, you can't.

29

BARBARA: David, let Martin finish.

MARTIN: Whenever we call Sarah in the dormitory, one of the other girls answers and tells us that Sarah's in the library or taking a shower or in class or eating or whatever. She's never there. After an interval, she calls back.

BARBARA: There you are.

MARTIN: The last time we spoke with her, she said we were hounding her and we should leave her alone.

TRUDY: Can you imagine?

MARTIN: She said we were treating her like a child, it was embarrassing her in front of her friends to have her parents calling twice a day.

BARBARA: Well, I'm sure it is embarrassing to her.

TRUDY: Oh, please! Let Sarah run amuck. She's eighteen years old, right? She's old enough—tell me that.

BARBARA: It's true.

MARTIN: She also said that we were keeping tabs on her and that she resented it.

BARBARA: What time do you usually call?

TRUDY: In the morning around seven-thirty; at night, around eleven.

DAVID: And she got the impression you were keeping tabs?

MARTIN: Last Wednesday, we called her at two-thirty in the morning. She got very upset.

BARBARA: I'm not surprised.

DAVID: Was she in at two-thirty?

MARTIN: She was taking another one of her showers. That girl must be clean as a whistle.

BARBARA: She might have been out late.

TRUDY: A shower at two-thirty. We're supposed to believe that. She thinks we're idiots.

DAVID: Trudy and Martin, can I say something? I mean, really say something?

MARTIN: You've never been shy, David.

DAVID: No, but I'm flip, which is another way of being shy. You know, despite my nasty tongue, I do like you both enormously. You're family.

MARTIN: We appreciate that, David.

DAVID: On the particular issue of your daughter, however, I must tell you that I think you are both completely deranged.

BARBARA: I have to agree.

TRUDY: David—

DAVID: Let me finish. Now Sarah might well have been taking a shower at two-thirty, after writing a paper that was due the next morning, or after being out with some friends, having a beer or smoking dope or whatever you do in Buffalo when you're eighteen. And maybe, God forbid, your worst suspicions are true and she was not in the dorm at all, but rather in some boy's house, tipped off that you called by a comrade on her floor. I submit, "So what." I realize this is hard for you to accept, but Sarah is not going to be a virgin for much longer and indeed may not be as we speak. She is an extraordinarily attractive girl with, as I'm sure you recognize, the most *amazing* body. She is, I am quite sure, very popular with boys. You'll have to live with it.

MARTIN: Are you finished?

DAVID: I hope I wasn't out of line.

TRUDY: I wish it was just what you said, David. I wish it was just that simple.

BARBARA: It isn't?

MARTIN: *(A voice like death)* Sarah is living with two men on Bogle Avenue in downtown Buffalo. She hasn't set foot in her dorm in a month.

TRUDY: She hasn't gone to class either.

DAVID: *(Stunned)* She's living . . . with two guys?

MARTIN: We haven't slept in a week.

32

BARBARA: Living with, meaning actually . . . ?

TRUDY: *(Nods yes)* It's not that she's living with some boy and he has a roommate. She's living with both.

MARTIN: They call it a menagerie.

BARBARA: *Ménage à trois.*

TRUDY: All right. Well, you'd know that better than we would.

DAVID: Although it usually refers to two women and one man . . . one of the traditional male fantasies, I might add.

MARTIN: I see. Well, apparently Sarah is taking on both these characters—one named Billy from Syracuse, the other a Peruvian named Gonzalvo.

BARBARA: *(Reeling)* I still remember the Paddington Bear we gave her.

MARTIN: Sarah's last words to me on the phone were, "I live for sex. Everything is sex."

DAVID: *(Staggered)* I spent my entire life looking for a girl like that.

BARBARA: David! Christ!

DAVID: I'm sorry. It just takes my breath away.

MARTIN: I had heart palpitations when she told me that, as you can imagine.

TRUDY: He was white when he came back to bed. I mean, Martin's always white, but this was a *pure* white.

BARBARA: Does Sarah at least like these boys? Or is it purely . . .

TRUDY: She says they're very close.

MARTIN: She told me what they do all day. Quite a story.

DAVID: Martin, spare us. Spare yourself.

MARTIN: First, she and the Irish kid . . . *(To Trudy)* What did she call that?

TRUDY: Head.

BARBARA: Martin, I really don't want to hear this.

MARTIN: She has heads with the Irishman, then she turns around and has heads with the Peruvian. Sometimes, she has heads with both of them.

TRUDY: I can't imagine how she does that. Can you, Barb?

MARTIN: Then, after that, they go out for lunch.

DAVID: That was just the morning?

MARTIN: "I live for sex now, Dad. I live for sex."

BARBARA: This is absolutely staggering.

DAVID: I always thought Sarah was precocious, but I must say . . .

TRUDY: You encouraged this, both of you.

BARBARA: Trudy . . .

TRUDY: You told her to go away to college.

DAVID: I thought it was a good idea. I still do.

TRUDY: Martin, tell them what else she said.

BARBARA: Trudy, we get the picture. This is obviously very painful for Martin.

MARTIN: No, you should know it all. You always thought of Sarah as your daughter. You were her liberated parents, with none of the responsibility.

TRUDY: You took her to see that filthy Picasso show.

DAVID: Oh, please! That hardly opened the door to *this.* Thousands of people saw those paintings and went home to their wives and husbands and children.

BARBARA: Trudy, I resent the implication that we're somehow responsible for this.

TRUDY: I'm sorry. I'm upset. It's just been . . . Maybe I'll take a little scotch, David. Any kind.

DAVID: Of course.

TRUDY: *(Holding out her glass)* Just put some in here. A little. It's fine.

35

DAVID: Martin, it's a quarter of eight. You sure you won't take a little head start?

MARTIN: I've always been a disciplined person.

BARBARA: But this is a uniquely stressful situation, Martin. We'd certainly understand.

MARTIN: All the more reason for me to keep my self-control. *(David crosses to the bar)* She told me things. . . . You know what she said she liked the best?

TRUDY: This you won't believe.

BARBARA: You know, I find this more than a little masochistic on your part. Going over and over this debasing conversation.

DAVID: *(At the bar)* I agree.

MARTIN: She's your niece. You should know.

TRUDY: So you'll understand our decision.

BARBARA: What decision?

MARTIN: So at the close of the conversation, my little daughter, who once loved oatmeal cookies and milk the best, now tells me her favorite thing is when these two guys spritz all over her breasts. Then she grabs their—

BARBARA: Martin, please!

36

Act One

(A moment of awestruck silence. David crosses to Trudy with her scotch)

DAVID: Where exactly *is* Bogle Avenue?

BARBARA: I don't know what to say.

TRUDY: What would you do with a daughter like that?

DAVID: Wash off her chest for openers.

BARBARA: David, *God!*

TRUDY: It's a blessing to have a sense of humor like that, to be able to laugh at other people's tragedy.

DAVID: It's not a tragedy. Not yet.

TRUDY: She's not your daughter. That's why it's not a tragedy.

DAVID: Listen, I understand your concern. I feel very close to Sarah, and I'm saddened that she's doing this. But I'm sure that it will pass.

MARTIN: When?

DAVID: She'll get bored with it.

MARTIN: She's going to be bored with *this?* With two guys? Then what? Horses? Cows?

DAVID: Martin, I would imagine that any type of livestock would be a real long shot. I think she'll just shake this

37

out of her system and resume her life. And I think your leaving her alone would be a big help.

BARBARA: I agree. She's just flaunting her sexuality.

TRUDY: You think we should wait it out?

BARBARA: I certainly don't think you should call her twice a day. You should speak to her, tell her that what she's doing is giving her a distorted view of sex, but don't be a scold about it.

DAVID: If she was involved with drugs, I'd be more concerned.

(Martin and Trudy nod thoughtfully)

TRUDY: We appreciate your advice. Really.

MARTIN: Trudy and I felt it was important that you know the background of this situation, so you'd understand.

BARBARA: Understand what?

TRUDY: Our decision.

DAVID: What decision?

TRUDY: I feel, and I know Martin agrees with this . . . *(Martin nods in agreement)* . . . that none of this would have happened if we had paid more attention to Sarah.

BARBARA: *More* attention? You paid too much—

38

TRUDY: Barbara, forgive me, but if you were a mother, you'd know there's no such thing as too much.

BARBARA: Of course there is. How can you say—

TRUDY: Let me continue.

BARBARA: I just disagree. I remember Sarah sleeping in your bedroom until she was, what, *nine?*

TRUDY: She had ear infections.

MARTIN: We had to keep an eye on her.

DAVID: You were far too cautious with her.

TRUDY: Please let me go on. We simply did not pay enough attention to Sarah and that's because of Mom.

MARTIN: We were preoccupied.

TRUDY: We were preoccupied with Mom—with her demands, her hip. As a result, we neglected Sarah.

DAVID: You didn't neglect Sarah.

TRUDY: Of course we did.

MARTIN: Anyhow, we're going up there tonight. We have our tickets.

BARBARA: You're going to Buffalo?

39

TRUDY: Of course. What do you think, we're going to wait until she's pregnant, or gets her throat cut by these two maniacs?

DAVID: You're leaving tonight? Did I get that right?

MARTIN: We'll be at the TraveLodge in Buffalo for as long as it takes.

BARBARA: What are you going to do? Abduct her?

TRUDY: Whatever you want to call it. We're being responsible is what I call it.

MARTIN: It won't be easy, we both know that. We may be up there for a month or so. I've already told my firm.

BARBARA: And what about Mom? *(Dead silence)* David, could I have another drink?

TRUDY: We can't have Mom anymore. At least not for now. We've done our share. We've paid for it.

BARBARA: But she loves it with you in Mineola. The garden . . . her room . . .

DAVID: *(Returning with Barbara's drink)* You're not putting her in a home.

MARTIN: She won't go to a home.

TRUDY: And I don't want her in one. She's not feeble, or senile. . . .

40

BARBARA: Trudy, what exactly are you saying?

TRUDY: You know what I'm saying.

BARBARA: I know what you're saying, but I want to hear you say it.

TRUDY: There's no choice, Barb. She's got to live here.

BARBARA: It's impossible. I'm at the gallery every day. I work.

TRUDY: Hire someone to be with her.

BARBARA: You said she won't have anyone.

TRUDY: Maybe it'll be different with you. *(Smiles broadly)*

MARTIN: *(Also beaming)* Yeah. Fat chance, huh, Trude?

TRUDY: Wait till she tries.

(Martin and Trudy enjoy a good laugh)

DAVID: Besides the fact that Barbara has to be at the gallery every day, we simply don't have any space here.

MARTIN: You have an extra bedroom.

DAVID: It's a guest room.

TRUDY: Well, now you have a guest.

41

BARBARA: Artists stay there when they're in New York. It was designed for that.

DAVID: Salvador Dali once slept in that room.

MARTIN: You've got a couch here.

DAVID: Martin, do you seriously think I'm going to put Salvador Dali up on the living room couch?

MARTIN: Artists are supposed to suffer a little.

DAVID: Not when they're eighty-five for crissakes!

BARBARA: Trudy, listen. You go to Buffalo, stay for as long as you have to. We'll hire someone to be with Mom twenty-four hours a day. On weekends, we'll go out and visit. I'll call her twice a day.

TRUDY: No.

BARBARA: *Why not?*

TRUDY: Don't yell, Barb.

BARBARA: Well, why not? It's a good idea.

DAVID: An excellent idea. Your mother will be happier; she'll have company all day. She won't have to be transported into the city, which can't be any good for her hip—

MARTIN: No, she did fine.

(David and Barbara freeze)

DAVID: She did *what* fine?

MARTIN: Made the trip in. Didn't she, Trude?

TRUDY: No problem. Her hip is like new.

BARBARA: When did she make the trip in?

TRUDY: This evening.

BARBARA: You brought her with you? Tonight?

MARTIN: Of course. We're going from here straight to the airport.

DAVID: This isn't happening.

BARBARA: *You just brought Mom in without asking us?*

TRUDY: What's to ask? She's your mother as much as mine.

DAVID: Wait a second. Where is she? You've been up here for forty minutes.

TRUDY: She's in the car.

MARTIN: We gave the doorman three dollars to watch her.

BARBARA: *(In shock)* You brought her with you tonight.

43

TRUDY: She's had her dinner already; you don't have to worry about that.

DAVID: *(Lighting a cigar)* Is she in her jammies, ready for bed?

TRUDY: David, I'm sorry, but you know, cigar smoke . . . the smell . . .

DAVID: Tough shit.

MARTIN: David, that's out of line.

DAVID: *That's* out of line? *That's* out of line?

MARTIN: David . . .

DAVID: You show up out of the blue, accuse us of contributing to the delinquency of your daughter, drink our ginger ale, and then, without consultation, without a word, you simply tell us that Sophie is downstairs, ready to move in with us. I have never in my life heard of anything so outrageous.

TRUDY: This is an emergency situation, David. We don't have time to argue. Our daughter is drowning, and Mom has to stay here. That's all.

MARTIN: *(Heading toward the front door)* I'll get her.

DAVID: Wait a minute!

TRUDY: We can't wait; we have a ten o'clock flight. Martin—

DAVID: You're just dumping her here, with all her belongings?

MARTIN: She doesn't have that much.

TRUDY: It's mostly medication, some clothes, nightgowns, a case of sour balls. Martin, hurry!

MARTIN: You ought to help me, Trude. Be faster.

TRUDY: *(Heading for the front door)* We'll be back soon. Barb, put up some tea. I know she'll want some.

BARBARA: *(Sinks to the floor)* She takes it with milk?

TRUDY: A single teaspoon of milk. More than that and she pours it down the sink. Also, not too hot. She burns her tongue. You have any pound cake?

BARBARA: I think so.

TRUDY: She likes a piece before she goes to bed. Toasted.

MARTIN: *(At the front door)* Trudy!

TRUDY: Coming.

DAVID: She knows about this?

TRUDY: Of course. "Now I'm living with my fancy daughter." She's very excited.

(Trudy and Martin exit, quickly. A moment of stunned silence)

45

BARBARA: Oh, God . . . David . . .

DAVID: It's temporary. We'll hire someone.

BARBARA: They said she won't . . .

DAVID: *They* said. *They* said! Those two assholes? How they run their miserable life is their business. If your mother's unbearable, if she threatens your mental health, we'll put her in the DeWitt Home.

BARBARA: Come on, that's five thousand a month.

DAVID: I'll sell some forgeries. It'd be worth it.

BARBARA: The thing is . . . eventually, they'll want her back.

DAVID: Absolutely. They need Sophie. Without her, they have nothing to talk about.

BARBARA: God . . .

DAVID: Scenario: they go to Buffalo. Sarah tells them to screw off. They return abject.

BARBARA: No, they'll bring her back.

DAVID: I can't see how.

BARBARA: No, I know them. Once they're pushed past a certain point . . . I mean, Martin's a schlemiel, but he can be a determined schlemiel.

DAVID: He gets set on something . . .

BARBARA: Exactly.

DAVID: All right. . . . So they bring Sarah back and keep her a month or so, say, until she promises to rededicate herself to the Great Books program and never again blow more than one Peruvian at a time. Bingo, she returns to Buffalo; Trudy and Martin return to long silences over the dinner table. They beg for Sophie's return.

BARBARA: That's your scenario.

DAVID: That's it. Sophie'll be here for one month, tops.

BARBARA: Maybe. *(Gets up; hurries to the kitchen)* Have to make that tea.

DAVID: Just because Trudy said so, you just hop to it? Your mother can wait a couple of minutes for her goddamn tea.

BARBARA: She always liked it the second she came in.

DAVID: Well, she's going to have to learn—

BARBARA: David, please don't start. Don't make it harder.

DAVID: I'm not making it harder. *(He follows her into the kitchen)*

47

DAVID: *(Offstage)* I just won't let you become a galley slave to Sophie.

BARBARA: *(Offstage)* I won't. I assure you. But she gets very testy if her tea isn't right there.

DAVID: *(Offstage)* I will not permit you—

BARBARA: *(Emerges from kitchen; David following)* David, just be supportive. That's all I ask. It's going to be tough enough. What I need now are support and understanding.

DAVID: Listen, I'm not going to attack the woman.

BARBARA: Things are going to happen. It's inevitable. I have not lived in the same house with my mother in twenty-three years. . . .

DAVID: I recognize that. . . .

(The thumping of a walker is heard in the hallway)

MARTIN: *(From the hallway)* Beautiful hallway, huh, Mom?

BARBARA: Oh, my God.

DAVID: How'd they make it so fast?

BARBARA: Oh, my God! *(The front door buzzer sounds)* David, you . . . please! *(David doesn't move)*

DAVID: She's your mother.

48

Act One

BARBARA: Please! I can't handle her right at the door! *(The front door buzzer sounds)* David, *please!*

DAVID: Okay. But just remember that I got the door first.

(The front door buzzer sounds, more insistently. David opens the door. A chrome walker thumps into the room, followed by Sophie. She looks at David, then slowly turns her glare to Barbara as . . .

THE CURTAIN FALLS)

Marlo Thomas and Ron Silver

Joanne Gleason, Marlo Thomas, Kenneth Walsh and Ron Silver

Ron Silver and
Marlo Thomas

Olympia Dukakis and Marlo Thomas

Stefan Schnabel, Ron Silver, Marlo Thomas and Olympia Dukakis

ACT TWO

ACT II

SCENE ONE

The Kahn apartment. It is early evening, two weeks later. Barbara, in slip and robe, is slumped in a chair, seemingly unconscious. The dining table is unset, but napkins, silverware, glassware, floral bouquets are in evidence. The living room shows evidences of the new occupant—TV Guides, old Sunday supplements. . . .

The telephone is ringing. Barbara awakens, reaches for the phone.

BARBARA: *(Into phone)* Hello? Oh, hi, darling . . . What . . . Oh, I sort of dozed off. Mother was napping and I took the opportunity . . . How is she today? Impossible. Just impossible. Oh, I forgot to pick up *People* magazine, that set off a wave of hostility; then we had a major set-to on the topic of house brands versus name brands, following her keen-eyed discovery of a can of Le Sueur peas in the kitchen. "A dollar nine," she exclaimed, "I didn't know I was living with Elizabeth Taylor." Well, you asked, David. . . . What? What slight change . . . You're leaving *now?* You told me eight, David, *eight.* No, of course, if Maurice prefers . . . *(She begins to straighten the room up, somewhat frantically)* . . . but God, I have to get Mother up immediately. David, don't start . . . She has to be with us this evening. I will not keep her in her room under any circumstances. . . . Well, explain it to Maurice, my God, the man is ninety-eight years old, he should understand. . . . David, take him out alone to dinner if you prefer. . . . No, I won't come along, David, this is my mother we're talking about. She's eating with us, pe-

53

riod. *(A dull thump is heard from the guest room)* She's up. *(Thumping)* Do not ask for whom the walker thumps, it thumps for thee. . . . She draws ever closer. . . . David . . . Yes, I'll wear your favorite dress. . . . Yes, I'll look sexy. . . . *Feel* sexy? No. I'm sorry, it's just impossible for me as long as she's here. . . . What can I tell you.

(The guest room door opens, and the walker emerges, followed by Sophie, her hair wild and uncombed, attired in a bathrobe adorned by a single embroidered rose)

BARBARA: Well, look who's up after the most enormous nap. *(Points to cordless phone)* I'm on with David, Mother. *(Into phone, continuing in this nervous, jollying tone)* Yes, she's had quite the little snooze, and I think she's in a somewhat better mood? Not so jumpy, we all hope? *(To Sophie)* Ready for a great evening?

SOPHIE: I didn't sleep a wink.

BARBARA: Of course you did. I went in there. You were out like a light.

SOPHIE: Who could sleep with that picture over the bed?

BARBARA: The Rauschenberg?

SOPHIE: Pieces of string and old newspapers—that's a picture?

BARBARA: It's called a collage. *(Into the phone)* I'm not picking a fight with her, David.

54

SOPHIE: To me it's no picture.

BARBARA: David says hello, Mother. *(Sophie nods, just barely)* And she says hi back. Okay, darling, we'll expect you and Mr. Maurice Koenig in just a few minutes. *(Hanging up the phone)* Well, I was wrong, Mother. They're leaving now.

SOPHIE: What?

BARBARA: *I said they're leaving now!*

SOPHIE: Who?

BARBARA: David and Maurice Koenig, Mother. I thought they were coming at eight, but Maurice apparently . . . well, he got in on Monday, and perhaps he's still a little jet-lagged. . . . In any case, I think our number one priority is to get you dressed and all spiffed up.

SOPHIE: *(Holding up a butter knife from the dining table)* Where did you get these?

BARBARA: Those? Georg Jensen.

SOPHIE: What?

BARBARA: *Georg Jensen.*

SOPHIE: Just like the ones we had.

BARBARA: Did we have butter knives? Isn't that odd, I have no recollection.

55

SOPHIE: Call Trudy. She'll remember the beautiful butter knives we had.

BARBARA: Next time I speak to her.

SOPHIE: The pattern was a little different. It was called the Loch Sheldrake Arms Pattern—after the hotel we went to, remember?

BARBARA: I don't actually.

SOPHIE: You don't remember the Loch Sheldrake Arms?

BARBARA: How old was I?

SOPHIE: Two and a half.

BARBARA: *Well.* How could I remember that?

SOPHIE: We stayed in the new wing, even. You have any idea what that cost? Even in those days, so you'd have a breath of fresh air?

BARBARA: Mother, I'm not disputing that we stayed there, or that it was a sacrifice. I simply don't *recall* the event.

SOPHIE: They had the new wing and the old wing. Your father and I stood at the front desk, and guess what he said, even if it cost more?

BARBARA: That we should stay in the new wing.

SOPHIE: What?

BARBARA: *That we should stay in the new wing!*

SOPHIE: That we should stay in the new wing.

BARBARA: Mother, I think it's wonderful that you did that for us—

SOPHIE: And those melon balls you were so crazy about?

BARBARA: What.

SOPHIE: You don't remember those either?

BARBARA: I was two and a half. How am I going to remember melon balls from 1946? *(Sophie shakes her head in disbelief)* What. *(More shaking)* Mother, why are you shaking your head?

SOPHIE: No reason.

BARBARA: There must be a reason.

SOPHIE: It's just amazing to me what happens.

BARBARA: Meaning what?

SOPHIE: How people change.

BARBARA: "People"? Anyone specific?

SOPHIE: What?

BARBARA: I said, are you referring to anyone specific? I mean, if you're talking about people in general, perhaps it's true, perhaps they change. If you're talking, say, about *me,* your daughter, I'd like to know what you mean. How have I changed?

SOPHIE: There's no reason to analyze everything.

BARBARA: I'm not analyzing anything. I'd just like to know—

SOPHIE: Nobody's changed, everything's nice. *(Studying the hors d'oeuvres tray on the coffee table)* Does this look gorgeous.

BARBARA: Mother, we really have to get you ready. . . .

SOPHIE: This is a fish, Bobbsy?

BARBARA: Yes. It's a cold mousse of pike. I have a Pernod sauce I can use with it.

SOPHIE: *(After studying the fish)* So it's gefilte fish.

BARBARA: "So it's gefilte fish"? No, I just told you what it is: it's a cold mousse of pike, and if people want, I can add a Pernod sauce.

SOPHIE: To me it looks like gefilte fish.

BARBARA: Well, there might be a family resemblance, but the dish is called pike. Cold mousse of pike.

SOPHIE: You wouldn't serve gefilte fish, is that it?

BARBARA: It's not that I *wouldn't* serve it; it's just that I don't find it a particularly festive dish. I'm not ashamed

58

of it, if that's . . . *(Sophie is shaking her head again)*
What . . . *(More shaking) Stop shaking your head!*

SOPHIE: Why are you getting so upset?

BARBARA: I'm getting so upset because in five minutes
Maurice Koenig, the creator of Yonkel the Matchmaker,
the windows of Masada, and the Jerusalem tapestries, is
going to walk into our apartment for dinner. Instead of
excitedly getting ready to meet this legendary, marvelous human being, you choose to sit here sniping at me.

SOPHIE: "Sniping." Please . . .

BARBARA: Sniping. What else is it? For two weeks now, I
feel like I'm up before some kind of review board. Every day, these debates!

SOPHIE: You want me in a home, just say so.

BARBARA: I don't want you in a home. I wouldn't allow
you in a home. What I'd like is a situation where we
could talk to each other without wearing flak jackets.

SOPHIE: You're overexcited.

BARBARA: I am *not* overexcited. Mother, enough—go get
dressed, please. This is Maurice Koenig we're talking
about now.

SOPHIE: Soon enough, I'll be gone, then you won't have to
worry.

BARBARA: Oh, for God's sake . . .

SOPHIE: "Sophie Greengrass, beloved mother of Barbara and Trudy, adored grandmother of Sarah . . ."

BARBARA: Stop it!

SOPHIE: Trudy had them all written out.

BARBARA: Had what all written out?

SOPHIE: My death notices. I found them in her recipe box, under "Casseroles."

BARBARA: Death notices? You found death notices?

SOPHIE: She had them all prepared.

BARBARA: Trudy actually sat down . . .

SOPHIE: She said that she knew when I died she wouldn't be able to think straight. So she wrote them out before-hand.

BARBARA: I can't believe it.

SOPHIE: Knowing Trudy, I thought maybe there was a discount, doing it in advance.

BARBARA: No, Mother . . .

SOPHIE: It was just her wish, I guess, right, Bobbsy? Is that the right psychological thing? She wanted it to be—

BARBARA: Mother, I think it was a dreadful thing for her to do. Inexcusable.

60

SOPHIE: First, I read death notices. The next thing I know, I'm dropped off here like a package from Altman's.

BARBARA: Mother, listen to me: I can understand your feeling hurt, feeling angry.

SOPHIE: Nobody's hurt. Nobody's angry. This is how my children do things.

BARBARA: Mother, you have every right to be angry. In fact, I think it'd be healthier if you actually *got* angry, if we could talk things out more.

SOPHIE: What?

BARBARA: *I said if we could talk things out more.*

SOPHIE: You'll always be my little Bobbsy.

BARBARA: Sure . . .

SOPHIE: In the ballet slippers and the tutu. Remember when we went to buy them?

BARBARA: Sure. On Fifty-sixth Street.

SOPHIE: Fifty-fourth.

BARBARA: *(Deciding not to press the point)* That's right. Now, let's get you dressed.

SOPHIE: I'm too comfortable like this. What's the big deal? Dinner is dinner. *(Barbara goes to the window*

61

and bites the drapes—hard; Sophie smiles in recollection) Even when you were little, you used to bite the drapes.

BARBARA: Mother, you have to change. This is a dinner party for the great Maurice Koenig. I will not allow you to greet him wearing that shmata.

SOPHIE: Even if I'm so comfortable?

BARBARA: Even if you're so comfortable. That's correct.

SOPHIE: Bobbsy, the man's a hundred years old; you don't think he'll understand?

BARBARA: I don't care if he understands. It is common courtesy to dress for dinner under any circumstances. Considering the stature of our guest . . .

SOPHIE: Your father was a painter; he loved me in my housecoats.

BARBARA: He was a house painter, and he did *not* love you in your housecoats.

SOPHIE: Of course he did.

BARBARA: He didn't. I specifically remember him walking through the door at night and saying, "Again a housecoat?"

SOPHIE: That was his humor.

BARBARA: That was not his humor. Mother, this is absurd. Please, as a favor to me, go now and get dressed.

SOPHIE: I never did you a favor? That's a good one.

BARBARA: Mother, I'm not saying that you never did me a favor—

SOPHIE: "Mommy, I'm thirsty!" Who was there at two in the morning with a glass of seltzer, Casper the Ghost?

BARBARA: You've done me countless favors, Mother. All I am saying now, as calmly as I can before all my internal organs explode and I fall dead to the floor, is that I would like you out of that housecoat before David and Maurice Koenig get here. That's all.

SOPHIE: Okay.

BARBARA: Thank you, Mother. I know how much you'd prefer to remain in your comfy housecoat, but sometimes these little social graces . . . *(Sophie stands up and slips out of her housecoat. She is standing in the middle of the living room in her geriatric undies)* I just know you'll have a fascinating evening. . . .

SOPHIE: There! I'm out of the housecoat.

BARBARA: *(Stunned)* What.

SOPHIE: Maybe he'll paint me like this. What do you think, Bobbsy?

BARBARA: What do I think? Mother, what are you doing?

63

SOPHIE: Having a little fun.

BARBARA: This isn't a little fun! This is psychopathic behavior!

SOPHIE: I thought you liked a joke.

BARBARA: This isn't a joke! This is pure hostility. To sit there half-naked . . .

SOPHIE: Trudy, I would never do this to. She has no sense of humor. But you, Bobbsy . . .

BARBARA: *Get dressed!*

SOPHIE: One of the benefits of old age, darling—you're less tense about things.

(The front door opens; Maurice Koenig, ninety-eight and natty, enters, followed by David. David stares at Sophie in horror)

DAVID: Maurice, this way. *(David opens the closet door)*

MAURICE: David, this is a closet.

DAVID: What?

MAURICE: It's a lovely closet, but it's a closet.

(David pushes Maurice into the closet and closes the door)

BARBARA: Thank you, Mother. Thank you very much. Mr. Koenig was just led into a closet.

SOPHIE: I'll wear the black dress, okay, darling? Will that make you happy?

(David rushes into the living room, picks Sophie up in his arms)

DAVID: What the hell is going on here? *(He begins carrying Sophie toward the guest bedroom)*

BARBARA: You put him in the *closet?*

SOPHIE: Just calm down, darling. It's only a dinner party.

DAVID: Why is she naked?

BARBARA: *(Picking up walker)* David, I did my best.

DAVID: This is your best? I'd hate to see your worst.

BARBARA: At least I didn't put a hundred-year-old man in the closet.

(David deposits Sophie in the guest room. Barbara fairly hurls the walker in after her)

BARBARA: Again, Mother, thank you very, very much. *(To David)* Get him out of the closet.

(Barbara locks the guest room door; David rushes toward the closet)

DAVID: *(Opening closet)* Maurice. Oh, my God, what a terrible mistake. . . . *(Breathless)* The apartment was recently redone.

MAURICE: *(Wanders out of the closet, somewhat baffled, greets Barbara)* Barbara! My darling.

BARBARA: Maurice. *(Goes to Maurice, embraces him)*

DAVID: The low point of my entire life.

BARBARA: Okay.

DAVID: Rock bottom.

BARBARA: Fine, David, I understand. *(To Maurice)* How are you?

MAURICE: I am wonderful.

DAVID: Why was she running around naked?

BARBARA: *(To David)* Can we discuss this later?

DAVID: No. Later she'll be dead. There'll be police and reporters all over the place.

BARBARA: Enough. Enough! *(To Maurice)* God, you look terrific.

MAURICE: For a hundred-year-old Jew, I look terrific.

BARBARA: You look terrific for anyone. Come, let's get your coat and hat. David?

DAVID: I'm nauseous.

BARBARA: *(To David)* Can't we please forge ahead?

66

DAVID: Maurice, let me take your coat and hat.

MAURICE: Thank you, David.

DAVID: Least I can do after putting you in the closet. *(To Barbara)* She's securely locked in? No chance of a breakout?

BARBARA: She's getting dressed, and I will not discuss it any further.

DAVID: I'll discuss it. Maybe I'll call up a radio show and discuss it over the air.

(Barbara leads Maurice to the sofa)

MAURICE: Has been so long.

BARBARA: Too long.

MAURICE: Three years.

BARBARA: It's three years already? My God.

MAURICE: Christmas '82. We all had dinner at Moulin des Mougins.

BARBARA: I'll never forget that dinner. Here we go. *(She helps Maurice to sit on the sofa)* How was your day in New York? Good?

MAURICE: Very. The Museum of Modern Art has an idea for my hundredth birthday, God forbid, a retrospective. The entire museum.

67

BARBARA: No!

DAVID: Isn't it staggering? Picasso, now Maurice. They're calling it "Koenig: From Yonkel to Masada." We had lunch with Bill Rubin. He gave us the full spiel.

BARBARA: That's absolutely incredible.

MAURICE: I told them, if I am not here, proceed without me!

BARBARA: Oh, you'll be here.

DAVID: I think even Maurice, with all his honors, was overwhelmed.

MAURICE: Absolutely. To imagine such a thing . . .

BARBARA: It's so wonderful.

(There is a dull thud from the guest room)

SOPHIE: *(From the guest room)* I'm fine. Just a chair, darling.

MAURICE: And then I saw the show at your gallery.

BARBARA: Yes? The Oliveros?

DAVID: Maurice absolutely flipped.

MAURICE: The color.

BARBARA: Isn't it great?

MAURICE: Like Nolde.

DAVID: I have to write to Julio in the morning.

BARBARA: *(To Maurice)* When he hears that you liked the show . . .

MAURICE: Excuse?

BARBARA: *When he hears that you liked the show.*

DAVID: Maurice, some wine?

MAURICE: Wine would be lovely.

DAVID: Snookums?

BARBARA: Thank you, David. A big glass. Maurice, I made a little appetizer, although I'm sure next to what your cook whips up . . .

MAURICE: *(Examines hors d'oeuvres)* My goodness. Gefilte fish.

BARBARA: No, it's actually a cold mousse of pike, Maurice. I have a Pernod sauce. . . .

MAURICE: Gefilte fish, this is not served anymore?

BARBARA: Oh, no. Of course it is.

DAVID: *(At bar, pouring wine)* Of course what is?

BARBARA: Of course gefilte fish is still served.

69

DAVID: Oh, sure. A lot of new gefilte joints have opened up recently: Gefilte King. House of Gefilte.

MAURICE: I know you are joking.

BARBARA: You know David, Maurice. *(Pointing to pike)* You'll try some?

MAURICE: Of course.

BARBARA: Pernod sauce?

MAURICE: Thank you, no. David mentioned that your mother would be joining us this evening.

BARBARA: That's right. She was just getting dressed.

MAURICE: I think it's marvelous.

BARBARA: Well . . .

DAVID: Maurice and I were discussing the extended family on the way over. Needless to say, I was singing its praises.

MAURICE: In America it is very rare, I think. Quite sad.

BARBARA: I suppose.

MAURICE: She has lived here long?

DAVID: That depends on how you define "long."

BARBARA: Just a few weeks. She used to live with my sister, Trudy, and her husband, Martin . . .

DAVID: *(Returning from the bar with wine for all)* And their lubricious, full-breasted Sarah . . .

BARBARA: Out on Long Island.

MAURICE: Yes?

DAVID: Then they left town in a somewhat abrupt manner, assigning us the care and nutrition of Sophie.

BARBARA: *(Handing Maurice some pike on a cracker)* I must tell you, Maurice . . .

MAURICE: *(Tasting)* Marvelous.

BARBARA: You're a dear. I must tell you, Maurice . . . my mother . . .

MAURICE: Yes?

BARBARA: She has, how shall I say, a strong will.

MAURICE: Of course.

BARBARA: One never really knows . . . *(Maurice looks at her over the pike)* One never really knows in what precise direction she might go.

DAVID: I think that what Barbara means is that Sophie's not used to dinner parties.

BARBARA: *(Sharply)* That's not what I mean.

DAVID: Excuse me.

BARBARA: I just mean . . .

MAURICE: Yes? *(Barbara cannot explain; shrugs helplessly)* That she's your mother.

BARBARA: *(Taking Maurice's hand, gratefully)* Yes. That's it.

(The doorknob on the guest room door begins to turn violently)

SOPHIE: *(From the guest room)* Bobbsy!

BARBARA: Mother!

SOPHIE: *(From the guest room)* This door is stuck!

BARBARA: *(Crossing to the guest room)* No. It may be locked.

MAURICE: *(To David)* That is her?

DAVID: That's Sophie.

BARBARA: *(At the door)* I'm opening it, Mother.

SOPHIE: What?

(Barbara opens the door, and Sophie enters the room— without her walker. She has transformed herself: black dress and a gardenia in her hair)

BARBARA: Mother!

72

DAVID: Billie Holiday. We didn't expect you.

SOPHIE: Fresh boy. *(Maurice begins to stand, slowly)* Please don't. You'll be up all night.

MAURICE: It is my pleasure.

(Sophie steadily makes her way toward the sofa)

BARBARA: You're really okay without your walker?

SOPHIE: What walker? *(Singing)* "Ha-lo everybody, Ha-lo . . ." Remember that commercial, David?

DAVID: I do indeed.

SOPHIE: *(To Maurice)* It was a shampoo commercial. I used to sing it around the house day and night, right, Bobbsy?

BARBARA: That's right.

SOPHIE: That you remember.

BARBARA: I certainly do. Mother, I'd like you to meet Maurice Koenig. Maurice, my mother, Sophie Green-grass.

MAURICE: *(Kissing her hand)* I am very, very happy to meet you.

DAVID: Sophie, you look ravishing.

73

SOPHIE: *(To Maurice)* I heard all about you from my daughter. She was so nervous about tonight. I said, for what? Dinner is dinner.

MAURICE: Exactly.

BARBARA: Mother . . .

DAVID: The point is, here you are.

SOPHIE: Here I am. So let me just sit . . .

(David helps Maurice to sit. Barbara helps Sophie)

SOPHIE: Thank you, darling. Who locked that door? Not me.

BARBARA: I might have locked it without thinking.

DAVID: We're too crime-conscious.

SOPHIE: *(To Maurice)* Locked in my room. Like a *meshugena*.

BARBARA: Not at all.

MAURICE: Oh, no.

SOPHIE: Maybe if I was locked in, it was for my own good, right, Maurice?

MAURICE: Barbara and David are so fond of you, they overprotect you.

74

DAVID: There's been a wave of mother-snatching.

SOPHIE: Sure. *(To Barbara)* Is he a doll.

BARBARA: I told you.

DAVID: Sophie, how about some wine?

SOPHIE: What a face.

DAVID: Sophie, wine?

SOPHIE: Why not, David. How often do I go to dinner parties?

MAURICE: Live it up.

SOPHIE: Live it up.

DAVID: White or red, Sophie?

SOPHIE: What?

BARBARA: *White wine or red wine?*

SOPHIE: Maurice, what are you having?

MAURICE: Excuse?

SOPHIE: What kind of wine are you having? *(To Barbara)* His hearing isn't so good.

DAVID: Amazing.

75

MAURICE: I am having white wine, and it is marvelous.

SOPHIE: Then that's what I'll have—white wine.

DAVID: *(Going to the bar)* Done.

SOPHIE: *(Moving closer to Maurice)* A little birdie told me you're pushing a hundred.

MAURICE: That is an unchangeable fact.

SOPHIE: I would have said ninety, tops. You look fantastic.

MAURICE: I have had a very good life.

SOPHIE: That's the secret. "It's the circumstances, not the years." I read that in *Modern Maturity.*

MAURICE: *Modern . . . ?*

BARBARA: It's for senior citizens.

SOPHIE: An *alte kocker* magazine. But very interesting. Even Barbara looks at it.

BARBARA: What do you mean, "even Barbara"?

DAVID: Honey . . .

MAURICE: I am so busy. No time for magazines.

SOPHIE: You're still working?

MAURICE: Oh, yes.

76

DAVID: *(Returning with Sophie's wine)* Maurice is a painter, Sophie.

SOPHIE: I know what he is. *(To Maurice)* My son-in-law is some character, isn't he?

MAURICE: He is a very brilliant dealer of art. As is your daughter.

BARBARA: Thank you.

SOPHIE: I'm sure he is.

BARBARA: *(To Sophie)* "As is your daughter."

DAVID: Give up.

SOPHIE: My daughter lives like a queen here. He must be good.

BARBARA: We live well. A "queen" . . .

SOPHIE: That ability David has, that's something you're born with, am I right?

MAURICE: Good taste. Vision.

SOPHIE: Sure. *(To Barbara)* You thought I couldn't make conversation?

BARBARA: I never said you couldn't make conversation, Mother.

77

DAVID: Heavens, no. We were counting on your conversational powers.

SOPHIE: *(To Maurice)* My daughter and I had a little discussion before you arrived.

BARBARA: Mother.

MAURICE: Yes. A heart-to-heart?

SOPHIE: Exactly.

DAVID: Might I propose a toast?

BARBARA: Yes.

SOPHIE: *(Ignoring them, to Maurice)* You have a wonderful face.

BARBARA: This isn't happening!

DAVID: Might I propose a toast?

MAURICE: David?

DAVID: A toast. To this evening. To the four of us.

SOPHIE: Very nice.

DAVID: To our continued good health and creativity.

MAURICE: And to this wonderful idea, to have us all together with your wonderful mother, Barbara.

BARBARA: Thank you. *(To no one in particular)* I can hear my heart beating.

SOPHIE: You remind me so much of Sid, my late husband.

MAURICE: Yes?

BARBARA: He doesn't really look like Dad.

SOPHIE: He was a painter, too. A house painter. *(A look to Barbara)* I know that's not the same.

MAURICE: But it's an art.

SOPHIE: But it's an art. Bobbsy, remember what they used to call Daddy?

BARBARA: The Rembrandt of Dinettes.

SOPHIE: The Rembrandt of Dinettes—my Sid.

MAURICE: Yes? *(To David)* This is true?

DAVID: I believe he even signed some of his dinettes.

SOPHIE: When Sid worked, apartments weren't like they are today. They had foyers, nooks, moldings. Sid was so dedicated, he'd stay up all night worrying. "That two-bedroom in Woodside," he'd say, "I don't know whether to go with a gloss or a semigloss."

MAURICE: He cared.

BARBARA: He really did.

79

SOPHIE: You know how much he cared, Maurice? And not just about painting. During the war—something about Hitler being a house painter . . .

MAURICE: Yes? Upset him?

SOPHIE: Very much.

BARBARA: He had sort of a breakdown.

DAVID: Took to his bed.

SOPHIE: He just stopped painting. For years, wouldn't take a job.

MAURICE: Because of Hitler.

SOPHIE: He worked for a friend, Nat Meltzer, repairing radios. Then the Rosenberg case came along, and it turned out Rosenberg was a radio repairman. Poor Sid didn't know what to do.

DAVID: Sid took these things to heart. He was a sweet soul, really.

SOPHIE: He finally decided it wasn't his responsibility anymore. So he went back to house painting. That was really his first love.

BARBARA: He did love it. Went on and on about all the colors. He had this book, remember, Mother, with all the colors? *(To David, holding up her glass)* Another.

SOPHIE: The big book. Do I remember?

MAURICE: You remember well.

SOPHIE: Like it was yesterday.

BARBARA: I guess nobody's hungry.

SOPHIE: He had such pride in his work.

MAURICE: And you felt the pride also.

SOPHIE: Of course. So, I can imagine what your late wife felt when you showed her one of your beautiful pictures.

DAVID: How does she know Maurice's wife died?

BARBARA: I have no idea. This is so incredible.

SOPHIE: She must have burst with pride.

MAURICE: She was very proud. Very supportive.

SOPHIE: Sure she was. That's what a wife is for.

MAURICE: That's what a wife is for, Sophie. Sophie.

(Takes Sophie's hand)

DAVID: *(To Barbara)* Why do I find myself trembling uncontrollably?

81

BARBARA: *(Pointing to Sophie and Maurice)* David! Look at this.

SOPHIE: He's holding my hand, Bobbsy. What should I do?

CURTAIN

ACT II

The Kahn apartment. It is early Sunday afternoon, one week later. Signs of a destroyed brunch and a Sunday New York Times *litter the living room. David and Barbara are in silk pj's.*

David is hanging a new painting in place of the Ferragini. It is a painting of Sophie by Maurice Koenig.

Barbara is supervising the hanging.

BARBARA: A little to the left. *(He moves the painting)* That's it. Fantastic.

DAVID: It's as good as anything he's done in five years.

BARBARA: And it's my mother. *(She sighs)* God.

DAVID: Amazing . . .

BARBARA: I'm just finding this so terribly complicated.

DAVID: Of course . . .

BARBARA: I mean, it's wonderful. . . . But none of us . . .

DAVID: A romance? No. None of us . . .

BARBARA: Particularly with Maurice. Jesus. She's already talking about the show at the Modern, what she should wear for the opening. It's two years off, and she's talking

83

about keeping Maurice fit, you know, in such a proprietary way. "My Maurice," "I told Maurice . . ."

DAVID: It's staggering.

BARBARA: I get a little dizzy listening.

DAVID: It's such a shock. It's insanity, really. I mean, *Sophie.*

BARBARA: It's so unsettling. And now apparently they're talking about moving her to France.

DAVID: No! Maurice asked her?

BARBARA: This morning. I didn't tell you.

DAVID: How could you not tell me? He *asked* her?

BARBARA: David, don't press me. Yes, he asked her. They woke up and ordered coffee and croissants and apparently Maurice turned to her and said, "We could do this every morning at Cap d'Antibes."

DAVID: Astounding.

BARBARA: She just loved those croissants. Went on and on about them. How flaky. She said it a hundred times: "flaky."

DAVID: Do you think she'll really go? I mean, from Mineola to Cap d'Antibes in three weeks, she'll get the bends.

BARBARA: She said, "I guess I have a thing for painters."

DAVID: "A thing for painters."

BARBARA: She sounds positively girlish on the phone now. And she hears everything. *(She goes to the portrait)* You think I look like her?

DAVID: A little. The mouth.

BARBARA: I suddenly feel like *her* mother. Is it crazy that this picture makes me so sad? I mean, I'm exhilarated by it, and wiped out by it at the same time.

DAVID: You see yourself?

BARBARA: I see myself. I see . . . I don't know . . .

DAVID: What?

BARBARA: I just feel so totally *strange* all of a sudden.

DAVID: Sweetie . . .

BARBARA: *(Goes to David on the couch)* Oh, David. Are we all right?

DAVID: Of course we're all right.

BARBARA: You don't feel like there's something missing?

DAVID: No.

BARBARA: Really? We're married sixteen years now.

DAVID: So what?

BARBARA: So, I don't know. What's the point now, maybe that's it. Things happen, people evolve, and all we do is comment on everything.

DAVID: That's not true.

BARBARA: I just feel stuck. Absolutely stuck. When Mother was here, I had absolutely no libido. Then she rediscovers sex, and she's gone. And I keep thinking of Sarah in Buffalo, on fire with sex, just on fire with it. The two of them, sixty years apart, burning at different temperatures.

DAVID: And you're in the middle.

BARBARA: Buried in the middle, that's how I feel.

DAVID: And no kids, is that part of it?

BARBARA: No, that really has nothing to do with what I'm talking about.

DAVID: Which is?

BARBARA: I just have to find that fire again. Both of us do.

DAVID: Fire?

BARBARA: I'm talking about sex, David. Remember? Sex?

DAVID: I remember it with great fondness. *(He gets up and heads behind the bar, to the CD player)*

86

Act Two

BARBARA: You're getting up?

DAVID: I simply don't believe in hammering things out all the time.

BARBARA: You always do this. You avoid any kind of confrontation.

DAVID: I believe in going with the flow.

BARBARA: What if there is no flow?

DAVID: There's always a little flow.

BARBARA: You're putting on a disc?

DAVID: Bear with me.

BARBARA: I don't want music. I want to talk.

DAVID: I want to waltz.

(The sweeping waltz from Der Rosenkavalier *booms out into the living room. After some resistance, Barbara allows herself to be danced around the apartment by David. The dancing becomes more joyful, a hint of real feeling. . . . They stop, kiss, then kiss again. Pressed against each other, Barbara and David sink slowly behind the sofa, out of sight.*

After a moment, the front door opens. Martin and Trudy stand in the doorway. Trudy observes the action behind the sofa and shrieks)

87

TRUDY: *OH MY GOD!*

(Barbara's pajama bottoms are hurled at Martin by the invisible David. David then rises, his own pajama pants still somewhat askew, and makes his way toward the CD player)

DAVID: Jesus!

MARTIN: The door was open.

DAVID: You people ever hear of a doorbell.

TRUDY: We rang and rang. That awful music . . .

DAVID: That "awful music" is from *Rosenkavalier* and it's some of the greatest goddamn music ever written. Thrilling, romantic.

BARBARA: *(Crawling toward Martin, she finally reaches her pj bottoms, takes them from Martin)* Scared me to death . . . God . . . *(She flees to the bedroom)*

MARTIN: We never imagined. *(Checks watch)* It's one-thirty. . . . The man downstairs knows us.

TRUDY: Frank. The Italian man.

MARTIN: Just waved us in. "They're home," he said.

DAVID: He's through in this building. Finished.

BARBARA: *(Reentering; pajama bottoms back in place)* Have you two had lunch?

MARTIN: We ate in the car. *(Seeing the portrait of Sophie)* My goodness . . . This isn't . . . Trudy, look at this!

TRUDY: What? *(Seeing the portrait)* Oh, my God! Is that Mom?

BARBARA: That's her. Have you ever seen anything so astounding?

MARTIN: It looks just like her.

TRUDY: Very nice. Who did it, one of your artist friends?

DAVID: Maurice Koenig did it.

MARTIN: Maurice Koenig? Yonkel the Matchmaker?

DAVID: Mr. Yonkel himself.

MARTIN: And he did a picture of Sophie?

TRUDY: I guess it's nice to have famous friends.

MARTIN: *(Pointing at the painting)* There he is!

DAVID: Who?

MARTIN: Yonkel. Flying around in the back there. *(To David)* This must be worth a fortune!

DAVID: Fortune.

TRUDY: *(Looking toward the guest room)* She asleep? God, I loved her naps.

BARBARA: She's out.

TRUDY: What do you mean, "She's out"?

BARBARA: I mean, she's out.

TRUDY: Alone?

BARBARA: Not really.

MARTIN: *(At the painting)* Fifty thousand? I'm just guess-ing.

DAVID: Fifty million.

MARTIN: Seriously.

TRUDY: *(Going to the guest room)* Mother?

DAVID: Fifty billion.

TRUDY: It's Trudy, Mother. We're back.

BARBARA: Trudy, believe me. She's not there.

TRUDY: *(Peering into the guest room)* Her walker is in there.

BARBARA: She doesn't use it anymore.

MARTIN: She doesn't?

TRUDY: I don't like this. *(Trudy enters the guest room)*

90

MARTIN: *(Coming up to David)* Everything all right? The old lady didn't . . . I mean, she's alive, right?

DAVID: Oh, sure. We wouldn't let her death just slide by.

TRUDY: *(Reentering)* There's no clothes in here! Where are her clothes?

BARBARA: Trudy—

TRUDY: What is going on?

DAVID: Plenty.

BARBARA: Trudy, Mother hasn't been here for a week.

MARTIN: She hasn't?

TRUDY: Where is she? *(A grim smile)* You threw her out. I'm not surprised. With your way of life—

BARBARA: We didn't throw her out.

MARTIN: David . . .

DAVID: We have a major announcement. Major.

MARTIN: An announcement?

TRUDY: Barbara, please . . .

BARBARA: Mother is with Maurice Koenig. They are having what has to be called an affair. *(Trudy puts her hand*

91

to her heart; she sits down as if struck by a tranquilizer dart)

MARTIN: What do you mean, an affair?

BARBARA: They seem to be very much in love, that's all I can say. It's been the most amazing week.

MARTIN: So they're actually dating each other, is that it? *(David indicates that their relationship is of a more physical nature)* That's not possible.

DAVID: Sure it is. You know what artists are like.

MARTIN: How did they meet?

BARBARA: Here, Martin. We had a little dinner party for Maurice. He and Mother just . . . it was extraordinary.

DAVID: They just hit it off. Drink, anyone?

MARTIN: Tab.

DAVID: Lime?

MARTIN: What?

DAVID: Lime in the Tab?

MARTIN: No. Of course not.

(David goes to the kitchen)

BARBARA: Trudy, how about you, something to drink? *(Crossing to her sister)* It's a shocker, I know, but if you'd been here . . . I mean, they just keyed right into each other. After dinner, Maurice insisted that we all go to the Carlyle to hear Bobby Short.

MARTIN: He's the blind one?

BARBARA: The blind one?

DAVID: *(Bringing a Tab to Martin)* Who?

BARBARA: Bobby Short isn't blind.

DAVID: Certainly not. Nearsighted, perhaps. You're thinking of Ray Charles, Martin.

MARTIN: Maurice Koenig took you to Ray Charles?

BARBARA: No, we went to the Carlyle to hear Bobby Short. And when Bobby saw Maurice walk in . . .

DAVID: He went nuts.

BARBARA: He sang to us for what, David, an hour and a half?

DAVID: At least.

BARBARA: And he finished off with a Cole Porter medley that he dedicated to Mother. He sang, "You're the top, you're Sophie Greengrass."

DAVID: Sophie was glowing like a Botticelli.

BARBARA: I haven't seen her look like that since my wedding.

93

TRUDY: *(Regains the power of speech)* What about my wedding?

BARBARA: And your wedding. Of course.

MARTIN: So where is she now?

TRUDY: She's with Maurice Koenig! Martin, listen, will you! God! There must be something in the air here, or the water, some sex chemical. Sarah used to get all aroused here, you two doing God knows what in the middle of the day, and now Mother in bed with some old man, killing herself. It's disgusting, simply disgusting!

BARBARA: Trudy—

TRUDY: I can't even trust her with you for three weeks!

BARBARA: Trudy, she's happy.

MARTIN: It can't be healthy.

DAVID: Why not?

MARTIN: Come on.

TRUDY: How can it be healthy at her age. Her heart, her lungs, her hips for God's sake.

DAVID: I'm sure they're doing nothing elaborate. At their age, anything is gravy.

TRUDY: She must have gone totally senile here. We always watched her closely, kept her alert and well informed. . . .

BARBARA: Trudy, calm down.

TRUDY: God only knows what you two did to her.

BARBARA: Trudy, this is getting a little ugly.

DAVID: Listen to yourself. You're raving.

MARTIN: I have to agree with Trudy.

TRUDY: I'm not unreasonable. I can understand a little fling before . . . you know . . .

BARBARA: Trudy, this is no fling. She's thinking very seriously of moving to France with him.

MARTIN: For God's sakes.

BARBARA: I was on the phone with her for an hour this morning. She's in love—you have to accept it. I know it's not easy; I've had mixed feelings myself. Very mixed.

DAVID: But it's out of our hands.

TRUDY: Of all the things . . .

MARTIN: She speaks no French. Not a word. She'll be lost over there.

95

TRUDY: What happens to her social security? Her Medi-care?

DAVID: Who cares? She's in love with a great artist.

MARTIN: It's irresponsible.

DAVID: Oh, stop!

TRUDY: She needs to come to the Island and calm down.

DAVID: That's the last goddamn thing she needs. She's a new person.

BARBARA: David, back off a little. Trudy, listen. . . . I really know how you're feeling. It's awesome, it's confusing. Not twenty minutes ago, I was sitting here crying about it. . . .

TRUDY: She has a beautiful room with us, a color TV . . .

MARTIN: The garden.

DAVID: I believe Maurice has a garden. About nine acres in the South of France.

TRUDY: *It's not fair! Goddamn it!*

DAVID: Not fair? Trudy, what the hell are you talking about?

BARBARA: David . . .

DAVID: How can it not be fair?

MARTIN: You know, Trudy has an emotional side. People think of her as this cool goddess. . . .

DAVID: But this reaction, Martin . . .

BARBARA: Trudy? *(No response)* Trudy? What is it? Something going on here? Something happened in Buffalo, is that it? Trudy? Tell us, please.

DAVID: We haven't heard a word, not boo, since you went up there.

BARBARA: How is Sarah? Is it as bad as you thought?

DAVID: What exactly happened? *(No response)* She's not downstairs with the doorman, is she?

TRUDY: No, David.

MARTIN: It was made up.

BARBARA: It was made up?

MARTIN: What she said.

DAVID: Those stories, the spritzing . . . ?

TRUDY: All made up. Clever little girl.

DAVID: Really. Really.

BARBARA: My God. *(Laughing)* What a thing to do.

TRUDY: Very funny, isn't it?

BARBARA: No, but really, Trude. Can you imagine you or me . . .

MARTIN: She does have a boyfriend.

TRUDY: A rabbinical student.

DAVID: A rabbinical student. My goodness.

BARBARA: What a relief for you two. When I think . . .

MARTIN: She is sleeping with this boy. She admitted that to us.

TRUDY: Yes, but I don't consider that sex. Not with a rabbi.

DAVID: Quite right.

BARBARA: So . . . That chapter is closed. Sarah's fine— as David and I suspected she would be; you and Martin are back home.

TRUDY: We've been back for three weeks.

DAVID: You have?

MARTIN: We got to Buffalo that night, checked into the TraveLodge, and called Sarah. The next morning she met us outside her dormitory.

TRUDY: In the lobby, Martin. We met in the lobby.

98

MARTIN: We met in the lobby, then went out for breakfast. We went to the House of Pancakes.

TRUDY: *International* House of Pancakes.

MARTIN: *International* House of Pancakes.

DAVID: Right.

MARTIN: And there she told us about this boy, how she'd made up the other things and how we should leave her alone and let her get on with her life. We took the plane home that afternoon.

BARBARA: And that was three weeks ago?

MARTIN: That's right.

BARBARA: And you've been out in Mineola this whole time?

DAVID: Enjoying a little interlude. I can understand that. A chance to be together without the normal stresses, the phone calls . . .

BARBARA: *(Sensing the discomfort between Trudy and Martin)* What?

TRUDY: We have something to tell you. *(Silence)* Martin.

MARTIN: You're the one who wants to tell everyone.

TRUDY: All right. Martin and I are splitting up.

BARBARA: Trudy . . .

DAVID: Well. Wellwellwell.

MARTIN: Things over the past three weeks . . . they just came to a head. The matter with Sarah was resolved, Sophie was here. . . . We had to face some facts.

TRUDY: *I* had to face some facts, that's who had to face some facts. Martin doesn't want to tell you, out of some modesty, I guess. Is that it, Martin, modesty? *(Martin looks at his shoes)* That he is also in love. This seems to be the week for people to fall in love. Except for Trudy Heyman, of course, who won't even have her mother to console her!

DAVID: Martin, you've fallen in love?

MARTIN: Another Tab, please?

DAVID: Sure. *(He takes Martin's glass and starts toward the kitchen)* Nobody say anything until I'm back.

BARBARA: This is so, so sad.

MARTIN: You get to a stage . . .

TRUDY: If you're a man, you get to a stage. If you're a woman, you get to the garbage heap, the junk pile!

MARTIN: That's not fair.

DAVID: *(Racing back from the kitchen)* What? What's not fair?

100

BARBARA: Trudy was talking about the double standard.

DAVID: What double standard?

BARBARA: You know: middle-aged men going for young girls, discarding their spouses; the spouses completely discarded.

MARTIN: My lover is the same age as Trudy.

DAVID: You're kidding.

TRUDY: *(To Barbara)* You remember our veterinarian, Harvey Plotnick?

BARBARA: No.

DAVID: *(To Martin)* This is the real thing, huh?

(Martin nods)

TRUDY: He used to take care of Pom-Pom?

BARBARA: I never met him.

TRUDY: His widow—Ruth.

MARTIN: I did her taxes.

TRUDY: For free.

MARTIN: Well, after Harvey died . . .

TRUDY: You could have charged something. You know that.

DAVID: That seems to me to be sort of a side issue, I would say. I mean, if this Ruth Plotnick is the one . . .

MARTIN: I'm in love with her, David. There's not much magic left with Trudy.

DAVID: Yes, well . . .

BARBARA: There's no way you two . . . counseling . . . ?

TRUDY: We're already living apart. I have the house; Martin's sleeping in Harvey Plotnick's old spot.

MARTIN: We're about the same height.

TRUDY: You remember the Plotnicks' house, Barbara?

BARBARA: I really don't. I don't know these Plotnicks. I wish I did, now.

DAVID: So do I. . . .

MARTIN: I have a picture of Ruth. *(Martin rummages through his pockets)*

DAVID: Martin . . .

MARTIN: Here.

(Martin hands David a snapshot. David examines it)

102

DAVID: Uh, huh. . . . She's quite petite.

MARTIN: She's sitting down.

DAVID: Oh. And the man in bed?

MARTIN: That's Harvey. That was taken in the hospital after his first heart attack.

DAVID: I see. Not the most romantic . . .

MARTIN: It's good of Ruth, though.

DAVID: She's certainly smiling brightly, considering the circumstances.

TRUDY: Well, sure. She had reason to smile.

MARTIN: Trudy!

(From the hallway, we hear Sophie singing "La Vie en Rose")

BARBARA: It's Mother.

TRUDY: Oh, my God.

DAVID: Sounding chipper.

TRUDY: *(Pulling herself together)* I can't face her like this. I just can't face her.

MARTIN: I'd rather not, myself.

DAVID: You could hide beneath the cushions.

BARBARA: Go out the kitchen. The service entrance. The freight elevator takes a while, but . . .

(The front door buzzer sounds)

DAVID: *(To Martin)* Ring twice.

MARTIN: Thank you.

TRUDY: *(To Barbara)* You tell her what happened, Barbara; I don't want to give her the satisfaction. She never liked our marriage.

BARBARA: Trudy . . .

TRUDY: Please! And tell her she has to come back to Mineola. I can't make it alone out there. *Please.*

BARBARA: I'll call you tomorrow.

MARTIN: *(To David)* Give her my best. I'll call her.

DAVID: Sure you will.

MARTIN: *(To Barbara)* Good-bye.

BARBARA: Good-bye, Martin. *(To David)* This is insanity.

(The front door buzzer sounds)

SOPHIE: *(Outside the front door)* It's me.

BARBARA: I'm coming. *(Spying Martin and Trudy's glasses on the table; to David)* Let me get these. Jesus, David . . . I feel like we're the sole survivors of an earthquake. Who's left?

DAVID: We are.

(David opens the door. Standing in the doorway, leaning on an ivory-topped cane, looking like Nina Foch in a suit, silk blouse, and foulard, is Sophie)

BARBARA: Mother!

SOPHIE: Hello, darling. *(Sophie kisses Barbara on each cheek)* The European way. Hello, David. *(They do the double cheek kiss)*

DAVID: Sophie, you look absolutely radiant.

SOPHIE: I'm exhausted.

BARBARA: I can imagine. What a week.

SOPHIE: What a week!

BARBARA: Some tea?

SOPHIE: Love some. *(To David)* He's running me around, that guy. *(As David helps her to a chair)* Thank you, darling. The Whitney Museum, the Guggenheim Museum, the Frick Museum. He loves museums.

DAVID: Well, it's understandable.

SOPHIE: Sure. He's an artist. The energy.

BARBARA: I can't believe how you look.

SOPHIE: What can I say. It's been a dream. But I'm tired.

BARBARA: *(Going to the kitchen)* I'll start the tea.

DAVID: I understand you're leaving us for Cap d'Antibes. *(Sophie shakes her head no)* No?

SOPHIE: I'm going for a month, then I'm coming back.

DAVID: Back to the Island? *(A negative shake of her head)* Here? You're more than welcome.

SOPHIE: No, David. But that's very sweet of you.

BARBARA: *(Returning from the kitchen)* It'll be a couple of minutes.

DAVID: Well, Sophie's going to Cap d'Antibes for a month, and then coming back. But she's not returning to Mineola, and she's not staying here.

SOPHIE: He bought me an apartment at the Carlyle Hotel.

BARBARA: No!

DAVID: Sophie, you're a concubine!

SOPHIE: When he said it, for a minute I thought, I can't do this; I can't accept this. A minute later, another thought came to me.

DAVID: Take it.

SOPHIE: Take it.

DAVID: A very wise decision, Sophie.

SOPHIE: I think so. He's such a darling. So considerate, such a gentleman. So much like Sid.

BARBARA: I guess he is, in a way. *(Barbara returns to the kitchen)*

DAVID: When are you going to France?

SOPHIE: Next Tuesday. Have you ever been on that Concorde plane?

DAVID: No.

SOPHIE: That's what we're taking. *(A beat)* You never know when things will happen.

DAVID: That's true. But this one is for the books.

(Barbara returns from the kitchen with Sophie's tea)

SOPHIE: So, what did they do, go out the back way?

BARBARA: Who?

SOPHIE: Martin and Trudy. Frank downstairs told me they were here.

BARBARA: *(Handing the tea to Sophie)* Here we are.

DAVID: They went out the back way, Sophie. They're having some trouble.

SOPHIE: I'm not surprised. They splitting up?

BARBARA: Yes.

SOPHIE: Over the Plotnick girl?

DAVID: You knew?

SOPHIE: That's been going on for a while. I think even before the husband died.

BARBARA: I'm in total shock.

SOPHIE: When he started doing their taxes for nothing, I knew something was up.

DAVID: Trudy's desperate for you to come back to Mineola.

SOPHIE: I'll visit. I'll come weekends. I won't move back. She's got to do it herself.

BARBARA: She's a wreck. I never saw her like this.

SOPHIE: She's always been a wreck. She just never knew it before. This might be good for her. Then again, it might not be.

DAVID: I would say that covers the possibilities.

Act Two

SOPHIE: I've got to take a nap. *(Rising and starting to the guest room)* You should, too. We're all going to Lutèce tonight.

BARBARA: We are?

SOPHIE: Making a special dinner for Maurice; some kind of bird.

DAVID: Roast pheasant?

SOPHIE: Maybe. That's a lovely restaurant. We were there twice already this week. They have the most delicious rolls.

BARBARA: *(Going to Sophie)* You've been on a fast track.

SOPHIE: It's about time. They tell you about Sarah?

DAVID: The situation cleared up. She was apparently . . . *(Barbara shoots a warning look at David)* How much do you know, Sophie?

SOPHIE: Everything. She was apparently what?

BARBARA: Apparently just trying to put a scare into them. She's actually dating a rabbinical student.

SOPHIE: No she's not. I spoke to her last night.

DAVID: She's not?

SOPHIE: She made up the thing with the rabbi.

BARBARA: I can't believe it.

109

DAVID: So what's the story?

SOPHIE: The story is she's living with the two guys on Bogle Avenue like she said. I told her I was very concerned. She said she knew it was extreme behavior, but it was just a stage, just something she had to do.

DAVID: Jesus H. Christ.

BARBARA: Is she going to break it off?

SOPHIE: Soon. It was just something she had to do. *(Seeing her portrait)* That's some painting, isn't it?

DAVID: Certainly is.

SOPHIE: *(To Barbara)* You like it, darling?

BARBARA: It's overwhelming.

SOPHIE: Makes me a little sad for some reason. I don't know why.

BARBARA: I know.

SOPHIE: I can't live up to it.

BARBARA: Mother . . . *(Barbara goes to her. They embrace with considerable feeling)*

SOPHIE: You're a darling. A darling. This is all because of you, what happened.

BARBARA: No, it's you, really. . . .

110

SOPHIE: You had me to that dinner, Bobbsy. With him. And I wasn't being so nice, I know it. Maybe now, I know why.

BARBARA: Now that you're in love.

SOPHIE: It's not the Carlyle, you know, or France, Bobbsy. It's just . . .

BARBARA: I know.

SOPHIE: I'm still a woman. I'm still alive. *(Starting toward the guest room, then turning)* Take naps, both of you.

(Sophie exits. David and Barbara stare at each other)

DAVID: Well, the afternoon certainly picked up, didn't it?

BARBARA: The fire really never does go out, does it?

DAVID: It's good to know, isn't it.

BARBARA: It's extremely good to know. Extremely. *(She goes to the CD player)* David . . .

(She pushes the on button, and the waltz from Der Rosenkavalier *resumes where it had been interrupted before. Barbara holds out her arms to David. They begin to waltz, as . . .*

THE CURTAIN FALLS)

THE END

111